The sales book- Instructions to insight into the motivation quotient

What is a good sales book?

After all, excellence is a selling guide to the best version of yourself in real time. Each time you successfully sell anything, you're the proverbial cover of the book that sells.

So, what is the best advice that I can give to anyone selling- **Listen**.

Here's a true story of my first encounter with being a real successful salesman.

This is the time when I was in my native country, India. Living in New Delhi as a young boy of 16 years age. I remember taking a small loan from my friend's older brother for a valentines' day outing with my then crush. Once the day was over, I knew that I owed this guy some money and he asked me if I can help him with a new business that their family was starting to pay it back. They were starting a business making and selling shirts. I was told, to pay it back- as I got 10 rupees for each shirt sold, I would have to sell around 20 shirts to pay back the money I owed. This is long before there was internet or ecommerce, online selling, etc.- so I was required to go door to door or set up a shop in a busy area maybe a couple of times in the week to make that number. As shirts even back then were not sold without proper advertising or promotion and branding. Here's what I did.

The next day I took about 25 shirts in a big bag that I walked with to the hostel building for the renowned Maulana Azad medical college, (MAMC) students who were there from all over the world to be great doctors- they had mostly everything there except time to go clothes shopping.

I told the security that I was a management student doing a sales project assignment and he was sympathetic of me carrying a huge bag of shirts- he allowed me to go the first level where he could keep an eye on me, if I was out of there in under an hour and made no noise.

I was out of there in under 45 minutes with orders for the next time with all 25 shirts sold.

At 16-years-old -

I understood that to sell there must be a need and if you can help fulfill the need – you can sell.

I never borrowed money from friends again.

Communication is 'the 'key- in school you learn the language and practice the craft by understanding the vast range of topics by reading. The actual application is when you are learning to communicate what you want to say through your perspective.

The alter ego that is really yourself. The moral compass or the message or prophecy that you are fulfilling in the manifestation called- whatever you call yourself.

You are not everyone.

In other words, you are not being yourself when you repeat what you have been conditioned to say or have heard all your life. You'd rather stay silent. Albeit that you should speak, make it your true self, else don't bother.

Let me ask you a question.

If truly the opposite of speaking is silence- then what is listening?

To make up your mind anyway about what to say, stop talking and start listening to all the voices in your head and that's going to take some time to be quiet- ergo meditation as some say- and when you're able to hear everything that you have to say to yourself you will come to a point of silence and then whatever still needs to be said- will come out.

If you're already not deterred, read on…

Talking to yourself

We all are always, forever listening to the voices that are in our heads- no not talking about any sort of ailment here- it's just the part of the expansive design of a human mind. We talk to ourselves all the time. How you talk to yourself is the genesis of everything.

The human mind is a narrator, an endless storyteller. In absence of a reason, we create our own reasons to stories to perhaps give it a meaning that we understand. Imagination is a gift that needs to be given some thought.

You may say that while it is what it is- you will agree that every human being's experience of joys and sorrows are as their minds perceive the situation to be.

And if you can control the thought, you can control the actions.

Will it be helpful if we can govern our thoughts or sometimes just stop them from arriving in the first place?

Let's talk about that for a minute.

Here's a tip to stop thoughts- let them come and go - if you cannot…. go for a walk.

This book of life is from the school of hard knocks. A guide for anyone to go from self to self-excellence. Selling all the time.

Let's get started.

Through the known times - evolution of humanity has been attributed to the external forces and the ability to keep up with them changes and adaption to the new- as the key explanation for the survival of the species. Perhaps that, and the voice within, that provided the direction, guidance, faith and courage to boldly do what it takes to navigate all of it.

The new version is now more advanced externally and magnificently aligned internally- creating an abundance of the many and not just the few chosen ones. Personally & universally supreme- individually and collectively, all at the same time.

How to Be AGILE and What is DISCIPLINE?

It is ...

Preparedness,

Self-beliefs,

Time management and,

Practice. Practice beats everything.

It's like sharpening the saw, (reference: 7 habits of the highly successful people - by Dr. Steven Covey)

Even communication takes a lot of practice to become great.

Get your story right.

It's important to have a clear direction or a narrative to start with.

Assuming that you're able and aware of the language that you are communicating in.

Here are a few fundamentals in no specific order of importance- nonetheless it will give you a good summary of what makes a good pitch,

Focus more on the general framework than the words being used.

Story board to avoid traps, and always rephrase- to check for understanding.

Acknowledge/don't stop, to rephrase/explain as required- as most people just hear and are not listening.

Remember, there are No apologies without ownership- the key is to try to have a good rapport with others. I beg your pardon, or sorry I don't understand are the most common responses, pay attention.

If you try to be positive on outcomes and yet pragmatic on approach- usually there's a consensus.

As mystic it is - '**What**' leads the path and not the '**How**' - focus on what you want to achieve and if stuck at how- emphasize on how it feels- internalize - even day-to-day activities.

If you can achieve in the mind's eye, you will breeze through the tasks - through the mental-physical tuning.

In each interaction be genuine - respect your time as well as others.

Try to help others - not because of karma alone- also helps achieve COMMON purpose.

Address to '**how's**' by drawing fundamental principles and details from various ends- inside out, outside In, through foundational theory, by definitions, by trends, by design- in short, break it down.

As granular you can understand, so can you explain.

If you truly understand and have to rephrase it in 3 or 5 different ways- you should be able to easily, do so - something useful that can help is to set routine time to ideate and review- refine on a regular basis and not just pushing through your day at work will help- if you're not taking the time to pause and think you're not learning anything.

End of the day success depends on are you sinking, swimming or sailing in your own words.

So why is it important to communicate effectively in sales?

Money- it's a crime share it fairly but don't take a slice of my pie. (Pink Floyd's Money lyrics)

It's a known fact -

Each and everyone's income is generally based on the value contribution they make to the larger cause- so, the real question to ask yourself is, are you helping **create money** OR are you a part of the COSTS to operate/live?

While both have niches (perhaps for only 35%-40% top population evolves and sustains)- the others that unfortunately don't evolve may not survive in the race at all.

So, if even for survival its necessary - then to excel it must be imperative.

To be able, you need to be aware.

To start your journey to your best investment decision, in your self – do the following if you want.

Understand your place in the stack - as that'll help you truly create more value for others and in turn for your own unique self.

Humans are pack animals with a society that has a pyramid of power and associated rewards for each level. The higher you go the more the rewards and power, if that motivates you.

Pay to perform can be hugely rewarding to those who understand the power of selling and can mold their responses more meaningfully and customize to that specific person/ situation every time to get to the desired favorable outcome.

Due diligence starts at the very basic level- you start by reviewing each information, irrespective of the source- more so, you review your own work- each time.

If you want to lead- start by following yourself first.

Once you have mastered any tasks there are chances of oversight and typos more than when you started- as confidence is a silly master and is a better servant. Always check twice.

Critically reviewing proactively, will help you stay on top of the day and not lose focus and momentum arising from negligence and lack of checks- If you don't take charge of your days and tasks in detail- someone else will come to tell you how/what to do with your time.

The biggest mental and mood blocker if you ask me- as creativity stops and angst kicks in.

Try to understand the system that you're in before thinking about what you want to BE in that system - to be able to consciously take the charge of your own placement in the stack.

If you don't own yourself (your time) perhaps you're a slave to something/someone else- even if you don't realize it.

Think of it as- Awareness is a practice of consciousness and not a door that can be opened sparingly through random activities, or chants or prayers- it's an ongoing and constant dialogue with the self and facilitating the answers for self before others- unbiased and honestly.

The more aware you are the more effective your life will seem- as we are observing ourselves as well, all the time- doing it with the consciousness, helps keep emotions out of the mix.

Be selective of what truly deserves your unique true emotions and feelings. As, most other things are just illusions-in thought not in life most of the times.

They are all in your head.

See thoughts are like butterflies in the flower garden of the mind- let them come and go as they please- only track and chase i.e. focus on what you want to choose or capture on the canvas- what you're feeling about the thought gives it life- as emotions have the vibration and sense of it's being- ergo it gives an option to manifest and get real in your physical world through the conception of the 'said thought' via the inception of your **feelings** (life as we feel it).

Remember, everything has a shelf life even thoughts- air the pantry out every so often so nothing decaying, rotten or obsolete, outdated and gone in the past - lingers on further and stagnates the atmosphere.

Renewing your thoughts as 'this is **not** how I usually think'- and doing it consciously, may be a surprising breakthrough for many.

So instead of focusing on what can go wrong, channelize your thoughts on what will it feel like when you have gotten it right and how effortlessly and joyful it felt.

That's the true coaching you have to give yourself and do it patiently, consistently.

After all, you have to *be your first and best advocate and the last standing friend, always*.

Worth mentioning, that while the application of these fundamentals are universal - they have a very specific and unique fingerprint- each is not like the other- Irrespective of the external associations and tags- Like the animal kingdom- either you're a predator or a prey animal in a group - one's solitary in action and the other's lost in chaos as a herd- humans can review and learn- taking consciously on both traits makes the human difference- chase some and follow others.

Thoughts can be recreated, unhinged on how it happened before -anything you can think, you can feel -hence you can recreate.

The universe is mental.

As above, so below. As within so with-out.

Guide to creating winning habits and how to create awareness subconsciously.

Be like a fresh start in the next minute (not next day/week or year)

Take the first step to acknowledge the real and then accept that you can feel differently about it irrespective of how you have felt so far about it - do this every now and then for both ends of your emotional spectrum - ecstatic to miserable- and be aware of what constitutes the creation or dispersal of emotions (what thought in short specifically) - the extremes will be mostly things that are areas that are out of our circle of control/ influence.

(reference: Concept of circles of influence and control and out of control/influence- Dr. Stephen Covey). recommended reading this book at least once.

The concept of circles of influence and control is a framework attributed to Stephen Covey in his book "The 7 Habits of Highly Effective People". I have read and followed his advice for a long time in my career. It helps us understand where to focus our energy for greater effectiveness and overall well-being.

There are three key circles:

- **Circle of Concern:** This encompasses everything that concerns us, both big and small. It includes things like the weather, the economy, world events, our health, our relationships, and our jobs. However, many of these things are outside of our direct control.
- **Circle of Influence:** This is the smaller circle within our circle of concern. It represents the things we can influence, but not necessarily control entirely. This includes our attitudes, behaviors, choices, work ethic, and how we communicate with others.
- **Circle of Control (sometimes included):** This is the innermost circle, representing the things we have complete control over. This includes our thoughts, emotions, and reactions.

The key idea is to focus our energy on our circle of influence.

By proactively managing our thoughts, actions, and choices, we can gradually expand our circle of influence and create positive change in our lives and the world around us. Dwelling on things outside our control (like the weather) is a waste of energy and can lead to frustration and negativity.

Here's the benefit: By understanding what we can and can't control, we can focus our efforts where they will be most effective. This leads to greater productivity, improved relationships, and a more positive outlook on life.

In essence, the idea is to grow what is in your control and influence and eliminate or reduce what's not in your control/influence.

Everything is mental.

All starts with the inception - the seed- but first comes the desire, the intention- the thought.

Similarly, first there's a desire to succeed, before you succeed- it's all mental.

To master any task- take more time to prepare and do it without multitasking.

(Definition: mul·ti·task: multitasking

1. (of a person) deal with more than one task at the same time.

2.(of a computer) execute more than one program or task simultaneously.)

'Give to Caesar what belongs to Caesar - give to God what belongs to God- Jesus'

While speaking of Tithe- or taxes here- To me this also means giving of what we have- our attention/our focus is the most evident of our intentions and truly what we bring to the table. It is what we give.

So, it's important to be sure of what we think about what we want and how we feel about it- as that's what we will get back. Energy is rhythmic in nature- like an equilibrium or a pendulum.

How to not multitask.

To succeed learn to focus on specifics- mastery is doing many things with unique focus and attention to all of them.

In a work setting - anxiety and chaos comes from lack of attention and focus required by the individual to truly accomplish the tasks and most organizations are inundated with jargons- without consciousness, they promote glib like multitasking as a way to achieve success- however for being successful you also have to be focused.

So, to do it well- do it fully attentively till you are in a position to do it truly a new way without stress- your way. If the outcome is clear - there will be acceptance.

Seek to always define success in words that can be measured with some degree of the specificity. No negotiable definition that cannot be left to interpretation- universally agreed.

Numbers can be a good starting point as it can be really specific and not vague. 3 is 3 and 6 is 6 and so is 9- not malleable to individual capacity or will.

Common understanding of the goals and milestones - mapped in the main design or framework (of the project/tasks/outcomes/objective/achievement…etc.) will result in common agreements and navigate the path for effortless and natural alignments of the larger purpose or fulfillment of the desire through these quantified tasks, actions, goals.

Lesson 1.

Be SMART in your goal setting and review- here's what I mean by the SMART acronym.

S- specific - exactness.

M-measurable - quantification

A-acceptable/admirable - set standard of measure/ gauge R&R (how) and aspirational (what)

R- realistic (real) - opportunity driving scope driving action resulting in the outcome. Prescriptive bottoms up -rolled over.

T-time bound - dedication of efforts - time to review/revise and recreate - ongoing constantly- hourly/daily/weekly/monthly/ year on year.

Lesson 2.

Keeping track and checking on progress is the 'I' part we all can do consciously, willingly - despite uniqueness of self- it's pretty simple to align milestones, goals and outcomes/results if they are SMART.

This is the main action to start with.

To further advancement - Putting more details to create SMART goals, actions and plans will help enable them to fruitful closure.

Get details-oriented so you can analyze and refine better. Reducing errors in your delivery and creating the right brand for yourself.

Making progress is also understanding the desire- giving it a conscious attempt at life though your undivided attention, once done truly- it frees you from thinking unapologetically about it ever again.

You thought, you did it and now it's done- nothing unknown or nerve wrecking about it again.

How to create SMART

To define common goals, milestones and success criteria, here are some ideas:

- Ask questions to define the agreed standards and measures- ask as many as you have.

- Ignore rudeness if people hesitate- most people are still multitasking and are not good at it- asking questions to them maybe a sign of weakness- whereas it's your best foundation principle- your rock to create on.

- Document in data and details (numbers, dates, weight etc.) as words have many meanings.

- To truly explain the concept - try to write it down- if over 10 sentences - write again- anything less than 5 is mastery - when talking about them in discussions try to use 3 sentences at the most.

- Help narrow down patterns, definitions and accepted measures of success or milestones - simpler to say and do, is done.

- Map and track to a progressive target- helps clear aspiration to natural curves for progression than just vague ambitions.

- Create FMEA (failure mode effect analysis) and control plans to each accepted and agreed milestones/nuance. (reference: Six Sigma tools and statistical validation of data progress).

FMEA (Failure Mode and Effects Analysis) and **control plans** work together to proactively prevent issues in products and processes.

Here's a quick breakdown:

FMEA

- Analyzes potential failures in a product design, manufacturing process, or service.
- Identifies how these failures could occur, their effects, and their severity.
- Scores each failure based on likelihood, severity, and detectability (often called Risk Priority Number or RPN).
- Helps prioritize which failures to address first based on risk.

Control Plans

- Use the insights from the FMEA to define actions to prevent or mitigate high-risk failures.
- Specify what inspections, measurements, or procedures should be done at each step.
- Define who is responsible for carrying out these controls.
- Aim to prevent defects from occurring in the first place.

Together they:

- Proactively identify and address potential problems.
- Improve product quality and reliability.
- Reduce the risk of failures reaching the customer.
- Save time and money by preventing rework and recalls.

Essentially, FMEA identifies the weaknesses, and control plans lay out the defenses to prevent those weaknesses from becoming critical failures.

The method behind the madness, is just the understanding of the chaos better than the control.

- Get familiar with the ecosystem and environmental fundamentals that are beyond control and the associated impacts.

Again, what you truly understand is what you can change to your liking.

To address confusion- maintain clean documentation that you can confidently and quickly understand and then explain. Keep reviewing and refining as you progress - based on your overall development and progress.

Key to understanding - Communication.

Types of communication:

1. Verbal/Oral

2. Written

3. Body-language- including physical (if, face to face) and everything non-physical, such as- tone, speed, rate, words, emphasis, manner and finally understanding based comprehension of the receiver.

The only way to improve overall communication and general acceptance of your understanding of the subject matter and opinions is to focus on all these and also be mindful of the overlaying external factors like backdrop, noise levels and the medium or channel of communication (Internet, network etc.) As the outcome is dependent on many variables and may lose its key message or become unimportant and vague if not done again, consciously at all times- specially at work and professional places.

How to improve your communication skills: -

1. Listen- podcasts, media, watching films, TV, listening to audiobooks, are all beneficial content that allows for hidden progress- through listening actively over a period, the natural flow of the language can be easily gained.

2. Read- contents and books have many additional advantages. in addition to just being a better grasp on the concept of the language- there are more knowledge and information available outside of the digitally available media repositories of information & data available.

3. Write (including type) - any information received and shared via an email, text or letter as the channel of communication - has a different flair as it's silent yet narrating in the minds of the readers (untouched by the biases of pronunciations, rate of speech and other influences etc. conveying a stronger takeaway on the intended message for the eases of the receiving audiences. Individual stories have survived the test of its times mainly what is still written and reckoned over, along with the deliberate intent of the perceived adaptation or meaning of the said words to convey the generally accepted terms of the meanings that's available at that point in time.

Don't focus so much on words than its meaning- that you want it to mean.

For example - the word Fuck (socially accepted via freedom of speech in the recent times) has the interpretation of over 15 kinds

1. Fucking

2. Fuck this / fuck —

3. Fuck that

4. Give a fuck

5. What the fuck? (who the fuck, why the fuck)

6. Fuck all

7. Fuck off

8. Fucked

9. Fuck it

10. A fuck-up

11. Fucked up

12. Fuck yeah

13. Fuck no

14. Holy fuck

15. Fuck!

In short, words have meaning that vary drastically and will require concentration in the way they're framed to convey the intended overall meaning to the receiver by the sender (of the message).

Moving along,

Like any art form or acquiring a new skill, practice conversation - it's crucial to be able to articulate what you want to say without much deliberation and be able to keep it simple - as we learn to be more confident in our expressions verbally, imagination gets a platform to be expressed.

Taking voice notes and memos also helps develop more finesse over time - as we replay and redo.

The other part of effective communication is using words that are more easily relatable and have a common accepted general meaning in our day-to-day speech.

Many times, the attempt to sound more articulate or superior by using scarce words have a contrary impact as the receiver may not understand the true meaning of the message and can cause confusion.

On the other hand, if you can explain the most complex topics or subject matters in a very simple almost basic way- it enables the acceptance of both your message and you more easily.

Most people follow what they think they understand and hence can *associate* with it.

At work, before and after important meetings and reviews take time to practice what you want to say and use visual media as complimentary tools in the overall story. And what you can do different next time.

Reflect on the high points and low points of your discussions once it's over to make necessary changes to your style and message package to improve.

Deeper, deeper meaning of the unspoken.

Consider all the subtle nuances from the meeting, like- tones, energy, pace and emphasis on words, areas, in addition to the feedback received to decipher the overall interaction- more than words.

Invest in your communication.

The need to invest in communication is more now than ever as now everyone around the world can connect in some manner with everyone in this universe and can interact, learn and react to the information being shared, freely.

Apart from words mastery and eloquent expressions- it also includes keeping up with the latest tools and advanced technology to stay on top of the art and spend quality time to learn and adapt to the changing world trends.

For example with the advent of tablets, smart phones and personal computers - the hand written world has changed, the speed and response time/TAT (turnaround time) is now reduced to a few seconds or minutes in most cases- so if you need to now respond to emails, texts and chats - real time or delayed, it's a good idea to learn how to type and get comfortable with these tools. Using the new modes and channels of information exchange will keep you up to speed and relevant.

The inability to navigate through this mix effectively and proactively is either going to slow you down or give you wings to fly, higher.

A few tips for effective development of communications are-

- Learn to type confidently on any type of keyboards- real or virtual.

- Don't depend on 'predictive' and AI generated word recommendation to craft your statements and sentences. This is the biggest threat to creativity and waste of time.

- Write the overall email or message and then read it again for grammar, tone and general sense of the message that you're trying to convey - pause- edit it to refine further before you hit **send**.

- Read again. Then click send if satisfied.

- Learn to use free writing software with text conversions, that will give your thoughts speed to flow and get captured effortlessly. Think Remarkable handwritten notes or other software for reference.

- Learn to take voice to text notes accurately using your smartphones.

- If you work in an environment where the main platform for communications is via using the MS Office Suite of software and platforms- learn to navigate at bare minimum the 4 basics:

- MS Excel

- MS Word

- MS PowerPoint

- MS Teams

Additionally, there are many self-help videos and books available free of costs in most cases to learn these tools.

- The main reason to learn and get better at these communication aides is beyond just getting quicker in your interactions, it also helps make your time management effective.

The key is to be able to use the overall spread of medias, sources and influences to narrate a more confident message and give it your unique style of communication, with ease.

It's all about marketing- everything in some way is- always selling.

So, whatever helps you market well- sells.

To understand the fundamental principles of marketing we can look at what the subject matter experts say- I highly recommend to read more on the topic from materials developed by authors like Philip Kotler.

4 Ps of marketing - Philip Kotler

As Philip Kotler explains in his book Marketing Management-

"Marketing is an administrative and social process through which individuals and groups obtain what they need and desire by the generation, offering and exchange of valuable products with their equals".

Philip Kotler introduced what is commonly known as the 4Ps of marketing: product, price, place and promotion.

The '4Ps', or the marketing mix, is a description of the strategic position of a product (you) in the marketplace.

The 4 Ps of Marketing Mix consists of:

1. Product includes options, quality, design, features, packaging and other related services including USP.

2. Price includes list price, marked price, discounts, shipping costs and competitors' prices even ROI.

3. Place includes distribution channels, platforms, websites and other online presences, physical locations, inventory, and delivery. Also, maybe the place(ment) in the segment. NPR - CSAT included.

4. Promotion includes branding, content marketing, advertising, search, influencer relations, social media, PR, voice and sales- word of mouth- returns and resells included.

While in his growth models PK adds more components to create the 5 steps model and some more Ps to come up with the marketing mix that allow for a more strategic planning and outcomes.

Philip Kotler's theory of the marketing mix further includes seven elements overall:

Product, Price, Place, Promotion, People, Process, Physical evidence.

- Kotler defines the marketing mix as a set of controllable variables that a company (or an individual) can use to influence a buyer's response.

- Kotler defines marketing as "the science and art of exploring, creating and delivering value to satisfy the needs of a target market at a profit". Or a desired outcome again.

- These elements are often used when creating marketing plans and strategies to effectively market to a target audience. Based on their individual uniqueness.

As a young professional and a management student, as I learnt these theories and assessments- It helped me break down the key components and work on each individually and gain knowledge that impacts them- creating huge successes and accomplishments in my career.

The level of details and breaking down to smaller subsets help create more specific 'end to end' plans that have concrete outcomes that impact different elements.

However there's another- **P-** perhaps the most important one that compliments all these fundamental ones, based on my experiences.

And this is the one that can be channelized and help control the others more effectively- deliberately, with practice. **Personality**.

Personality.

Your personality is the metaphorical - the look and feel cover of the book.

Most people will make assumptions and perceptions about you and your place in the mix of the larger scheme of things- based on your overall personality and how you show.

I break down personality into 2 facets to simplify further- personal and professional.

Each interaction can be either personal or professional- cannot be both.

To be successful in your professional life you also need to be successful in your personal life- that's the law of balance and vibrations.

The first step is to be aware of the differences between the 2 parallel co-existing environments- personal and professional.

A very important way to think in the right manner is to not be too emotional at your professional front and not too analytical in your personal life.

Keep a check on what you're feeling and stay clear from judgment.

At work, pay attention to your value contribution to the organization - daily and comparatively better than the last time.

Again, you're on your own to gauge progress before others is a good thing.

The Art of storytelling

The ability to engage is the first step.

Keeping them engaged is the rest of it.

The real difference between a Master and others is the amount of time spent in practice.

Like any form of expression- and more so in Arts the key is the use of the unsaid.

The receiver (of the message) must arrive at the end message on their own and should be left open for agreements.

A true artist loves to create and then break it down into small fragments- to meaningfully recreating something more than the last time.

Like a constant refresh and redesign.

As a storyteller- the canvas is vast and open.

Each moment is there to help yourself get better. And how do we get better, by doing more of it.

Typically, a story has a foreword to provide context to the environment- then there's main characters introduction and what's the desired outcome for each of them- followed by their journeys to the moment of truth and finally, a summary of any specific key theme, emotion or message as visualized by the storyteller.

This main specific key theme, emotion or message is the fundamental narrative or perspective that the teller is trying to share. Be very clear about it in your storytelling.

The fundamental narrative is the most crucial thing- if that's unclear there's no story being told- however indirect and unopen it may seem.

The audience must assess the key theme or notion of the said narrative- to continue and to make way through the entire story once the narrative is set and agreed.

Else they lose interest, get confused and frustrated due to the ambiguity of the conversation and the overall purpose of the story being told not being clear.

As we practice relaying key messages to others with more accuracy in a short exchange with pleasantness - we continue to learn to master the art of storytelling.

Sentence formation and words used are a signature to each individual, yet they have a set limitation to their final interpretation and overall acceptance- generally magnified to the understanding of the key narrative- or in the context being shared.

In meetings, keeping an open mind to seek to understand first- helps in removing any barriers and biases that are preconceived and predictive in nature. To get better at the way to communicate is to practice with various people - one on one even in group settings- and to engage better.

As a creator of your impact and your unique way of storytelling- over a period of time, even others will contribute it to the team's success and how confidently and simply- the way you managed the narrative.

This is again irrespective of the individualisms that can be a barrier to most - now is a key differentiator and value creator for you.

In other words, talk freely, think constantly and express concisely- using very common words.

Word play is a game- it's just that- use it to keep engaged mostly.

It will however not suffice- key here still is the fundamental narrative- we need to focus on improving the method to handle the narrative in the way the story is evolving and create tangible and meaningful outcomes.

Just a reminder- everything visual, audio, implied and observed is adding to it hence needs to be delicately handled always .

Pay attention to the surroundings without being uptight.

The most important thing is presence of mind. Meaning, are you able to process, filter and operate in that environment (elevator/boardroom/ or if your business takes you to a fish market so be it). Are you able to still communicate effectively.

Here are a few tips to help develop the *invisible muscle*- to grow the presence of mind.

Consciously spend a part of your day alone- learn to spend quality time with yourself.

Be aware of how you are feeling first, if you want to manage these feelings and how you do in spite of them is the final goal.

A true master (or the best warrior) is never angry (Lao Tzu)- especially when faced with chaos and turmoil.

To be able to master any art- have an outlet - and use it frequently.

Spending time doing this thing/ the desired 'outlet' consistently, will help channelize mental energies and help create better outcomes subconsciously in all other dimensions of your life.

A controlled mind is a great tool- once the mind calms down the other levels also become active and accessible.

Breathing consciously and letting thoughts come and go- without attachment is the way to recycle and practice key messages that will help during daily organization.

In addition to being Zen mindset, staying calm - it helps us tap into inner learnings from our practice and past experiences and as we learn to use the mind as a tool- present - yet not rogue on its own free violation- the master emerges.

Say something, if you have been quiet to understand.

Now say something that it means to you.

Now say something that it does not mean at all to clarify.

Ask to rephrase and acknowledge.

Now move on and say something again to close purposefully. A follow up or conclusion is ideal at this point.

Learning to agree to disagree.

We all need to practice this more with ourselves than others.

We need to learn to say 'No' in the right way.

We need to learn to address concerns shared by others openly.

If the feedback is specific to a task, activity or outcome- retain it- as even if you don't agree and don't / may not like it- the fact it's out there means that you have an opportunity to make a move and or improve.

Magic is what you create when your desire echoes through your actions- exclusive desires.

Try to practice patience by being mindful.

Remember to breathe short regular in/out - helps you stay calm.

If you're the project or people's lead - Always I mean always, take the direct heat, don't pass it on else you have failed being the lead.

If there's a specific reason or person to be blamed- have a one on one and set it up formally alone and stay on topic- as follow up set a clear performance improvement plan.

Arguably you can choose your teams and assets wisely if it allows. Even then your blame is not shareable if you're the lead.

Always have a plan- even and specially for small tasks, activities leading onto the larger scheme of things.

Create a clear strategy- first thing is to align the team and stakeholders on what's the common accepted outcome to agree on for this strategy.

Then, call out dependencies and quantify the perceived risks.

Create a FMEA model.

Most eagerly, listen to others and take actual and mental notes.

Check for understanding when you're done communicating.

In each problem, in principle, there's a solution - ask to know what it maybe before you try to solve the problem from other sources or all by yourself.

Managing dialogues, most of the times, is also managing expectations (even higher ups) and to genuinely do well you got to do this right.

Seek to be a problem solver, people's person who can communicate and collaborate effortlessly- who is easy to work with and attracts favors. The key is to Never say No to help- without hearing the' asks '- also if you help- you get a favor back.

Clearly Ask questions, data and information required to visually see, where you can, the other person's point of view. Seek to arrive on consensus and unanimous agreements using data and visual media.

As a master of the art- it's really important and beneficial to understand '**the show me'** versus **'tell me'** crowd.

The 'Show me' crowd is the data driven, looking for logical outcomes and the devil is in the details group. You need to carry a lot of data and analytical fodder to fuel these discussions to a meaningful consensus.

The 'Tell Me' crowd is not too impressed with data and numbers, trends and patterns- they need succinct answers and open ended conversations to decide their position. Taking examples and references to storyboard your key points will be a good idea with them.

As a master seller, once you understand your audience is show me type- then you start getting maximum accuracy around your messages using data, graphs and analysis to gain confidence as the presenter and if they're more the 'tell me' type then present more specific outcomes and references without getting into complicated data and sets- where simple points and callouts will work better.

On a lighter note, yet meaningfully- 'Any fool can make it complicated and complex- it takes a real genius to explain it to a 3-year-old child or alike.'

Best practices

In daily meetings and conference calls- learn to draft as you see- most common in my workplace is using an empty excel tab or a notepad file to start creating as you engage and discuss with the stakeholders on the call. Arriving on consensus as you create with the team on what needs to be done and when, by whom and who's the final receiver of the result outcomes will help stay on track.

Adapt. Adapt. Adapt.

If you're not good at the basic tools- please take the time to learn.

Time Management

Learn to manage time effectively is next big thing to do.

The key to effective time management is prioritization.

A simple way to assess success is the goal that if the time spent in the value-add domain, is Important however not Urgent- you eliminate the need to rush and stress. Giving the task the right amount of attention and preparation will enhance the outcome and improve the chances of success.

On the other hand, Important and Urgent tasks will demand attention and eat into your schedule- causing chaos, stress and lead to unfavorable results and outcomes- mainly due to the lack of preparation and practice.

To finish off any task successfully you need to start successfully; to start successfully you need to plan successfully.

The most important planning for success is the discipline to follow a set routine, keeping all your mental, physical, emotional, spiritual and social needs met- both at the professional and the personal front.

Plan your day- block your calendar and respect it.

A simple exercise is to:

- Write down all the activities at work and then at home separately.

- Allocate time to each activity.

- Now assign urgency and importance to each activity.

- Create a roster for work

- Create a to-do for personal

- Start setting dedicated slots to each of these activities.

- Block your calendar for each one based on the order of priority.

- Assess your success in managing your schedule daily.

- Review and optimize for the next day/week.

- Self analyze the times that you were not successful and write down the reasons for the delay.

- If due to systemic reasons, try to work around it- if not, most likely its due to the non-value add (NVA) activities that eat into the times. NVA are activities like procrastination, water cooler chats, smoke breaks, social media or plain tardiness. All these NVA are deterrents to reaching one's true potential and efficiency goals.

- Success in managing or reducing the NVA will allow for more time to create and practice with a more relaxed and open mindset.

- Do this diligently and critically each day and you will succeed in your goals and delivery on time- leading to gratification and positivity- these are key to self-excellence.

- Happy mindset, Happy people, Happy results.

	Urgent	Not Urgent
Important	**I** **Fire Fighting** Crises Pressing problems Deadline-driven projects	**II** **Quality Time** Prevention, capability improvement Relationship building Recognizing new opportunities Planning, recreation
Not Important	**III** **Distraction** Interruptions, some callers Some mail, some reports Some meetings Proximate, pressing matters Popular activities	**IV** **Time Wasting** Trivia, busy work Some mail Some phone calls Time wasters Pleasant activities

Ref: The EISENHOWER Box below is a great tool to break down activities and tasks, based on their importance and urgency to develop prioritization at a daily basis.

A favorite example reference, to drive the point home for me was- Examinations/assessments are Important and we need to prepare for the tests- however if the tests are tomorrow (meaning important and also now urgent) you can't start preparation on it today and should have started sooner to get a better score and results. Such is the pragmatic reasoning for successfully managing your time effectively to your advantage.

'Time is the real currency- same for the rich and the poor- spend wisely or it has the potential to change both.'

Keep a vigilant check on your time- do more proactive than reactive activities to get more efficient with your time.

Another key component to navigate your day is keeping a check on what's professional and what's not- always keep personal outside. The job pays for your time, energy, vibration and service for the 40 hours or so that most commonly applies- if you're doing more than you're not managing your time well or the expectations from you.

Don't get emotional at work-only be Pragmatic and stay focused on non-personality reasons to address - if you're drawn to negativity and gossip- you have not yet embarked on the journey of self and excellence. Give yourself sometime and be aware.

In personal life, what you do when you're not working officially -Don't always be pragmatic, be emotional there- go to the kids' football game or dance recitals - work can still be done when you're back however the kids will remember the choice you have exposed them to.

If you're in the business of saving lives' even more a reason to manage better living habits and practice what you preach.

Like playing a game or writing or music that makes you forget about what else is happening in your life- a true release. *'The Inspiration You Seek Is Already Within You. Be Silent and Listen.' - Rumi*

Book smart or street smart

The real reason some people are more successful and happier than others is mainly driven from the internal strength that they possess. This is the reason I decided to write this book. I know it's going to help many young and old people based on their individual journeys - an attempt to light the candle within.

Most scholars and scientists have made breakthroughs in their research and studies driven purely by the instincts or internal alignments. The lessons can come from every source to the one who is eager to learn and knows no limitation. We just need to be aware and stay open to new lessons- even when we grow older in age.

As true learning is a lesson for many lifetimes and not just one- its an ongoing process. For simplicity and anyone who does not believe in many lifetimes from a reincarnation/ spiritual progression point of view- I also want to highlight the generations and life's that are watching YOU and learning from you- your younger siblings, children and even people around you at work/home. Be conscious of what you're sharing ahead.

Focusing on individual path to excellence is a choice- we can only choose ones we are aware of our options and the strength to choose based on our internal mental alignments.

The phrase school of hard knocks may mean to some as a reference for life- as you get the lesson after you get knocked out by it. However, the lessons that we learn outside of school, colleges and workplaces is perhaps the more intricate one that we can reflect on. These are the lessons that build up our mental strength, flexibility, rigidness and belief systems. In some context psychologists may refer this to be the differentiator to the norm- accredited - also called being street smart.

A real attempt to understand and learn the key lessons or fundamental principles of this nuance is very important for a wholistic growth and journey towards self-excellence.

The belief that you're in charge and in control to make a choice - real time (now)- drawing strength and guidance from both your academic (books) and our internal aptitude (street) knowledge or smartness.

The self-acceptance/mindset of victory leads to victory and defeat to defeat.

Point to mention here is that being street smart also means reflecting on your individual personal experiences and recollections to refine your own response to a similar said situation from your past.

'I have learned silence from the talkative, toleration from the intolerant, and kindness from the unkind; yet, strange, I am ungrateful to those teachers.' -Khalil Gibran

We all are constantly evolving and changing our minds and understanding of ourselves with that.

'If you think you can do it, you can" is a quote by John Burroughs.'

Henry Ford is also known for saying, "*If you think you can, or you think you can't either way you are right*".

This quote suggests that believing you can achieve something makes you more likely to act. It also emphasizes how much attitude determines success or failure.

As everything is truly mental and starts in your mind first- be careful of your thoughts. Thoughts of victory or thoughts of defeat- both are true- as you choose to think you will be.

A sportsman or a successful person may perhaps be lucky; if his luck comes from himself, as self-belief.

A simple way is to see if you're really adding to the problem or can you change it and create a solution.

To create new - be new.

Lessons from Chanakya

Chanakya was an Indian philosopher, jurist, and royal advisor. His original name was Vishnu Gupta, yet he is recognized for his pen name Kautilya.

He wrote 'Arthashastra' on the Science of Politics and Economics between the 2nd century BCE and 3rd century CE. He wrote books on many things such as ethics and statecraft.

For this discussion, I would like to quote his theory on readiness and response for success based on the awareness of the others-

"Saam, Daam, Dand, Bhed" is a Hindi idiom that translates to "by any and all means". It is also known as "Chanakya's neeti" (Chanakya's law). The four words are defined as follows:

1. Saam: To ask and offer advice

2. Daam: To buy and offer help

3. Dand: To punish for wrong deeds

4. Bhed: To exploit others by their secret

These are literal translations and would be apt to seek a deeper meaning in regards to these concepts - to get a favorable outcome based on your individual situation and the relationships at play.

Here's my interpretation and application to our business world now:

• **Saam**- stands for being the advisor/teacher to those who need guidance or coaching on a specific task, and it'll lead you to a leadership position. Hand holding such an individual will result in a quicker acceptance and arrival at the desired results and outcomes- additionally create a bond of trust and support. Be the teacher to anyone new in your team and create a network of people who deem you virtuous and worthy.

• **Daam**- stands for price or reward for success. As a leader, you will need to motivate others to help you reach the desired outcomes and results.

However, motivation is a very complex topic and varies by individually-Motivation as per Maslow's need hierarchy is divided into 7 different tiers of needs.

ref: Maslow's hierarchy of needs includes the following needs:

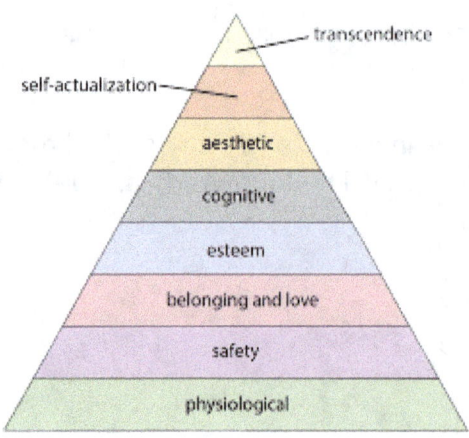

○ Self-actualization: The desire to reach one's full potential. This need can only be met once all other needs are satisfied.

○ Physiological needs: Hunger, thirst, and other basic drives.

○ Safety: Safety from danger or stability in health or money.

○ Esteem: The need to gain recognition, status, and feel respected.

○ Belongingness and love: The need to feel loved and accepted.

○ Social needs: A sense of social belonging.

○ Transcendence: The goal of human growth where an individual stops looking out for only their benefit but rather the benefit of humanity.

These have evolved over time however the main fundamental principle still applies both in Chanakya's laws and in Maslow's need hierarchy.

Abraham Maslow's pyramidal "Hierarchy of Needs" model is a highly influential way of organizing human needs from the most "basic" to the most advanced. Maslow's argument is that the most basic needs must be met before people can move "up" to the more advanced needs- And to motivate an individual it's important to know what their need is- what will motivate them truly right now. As an example- if a person is struggling in meeting his needs physiologically and you offer spiritual progression or self-actualization to them- the impact may not be fruitful. A true Leader understands his/her teams and will know what moves them and motivates for favorable outcomes.

- **Dand**- stands for punishment or correction for bad behavior or attitude and wrong deeds. This is the most important and confusing concept of the 4- the correction or punishment is not only to curb wrong doings and setting examples for others to understand the consequences and follow; it also needs to be corrective in nature not just punitive and limiting. The intent is to set up an example with a performance improvement or course correction mindset and not just abuse the title within the organization. This fundamental principle is still aligned to improvement and efficiency mindset- each resource is worthy and is required to make a larger contribution. People are open to correction and turn vengeful and distracted when the leader is missing what I call 'the care component quotient'. This is directly linked to your individual higher progression and takes conscious considerations along with patience when dealing with people who are not helping your cause- some may still need to go- however losing any trained resource or employee team members is a waste of resources and time as it will need to replace, onboarded, trained and will require a turnaround time to reach a level of error free proficiency. The other outward impact on this one, is your perception of being a destroyer may sound good initially - the task master and bullish leadership style will get early recognition- however over a career it will become a short stint as most people want to avoid task masters, more so now in the more aware connected and AI driven world. After all- perception is sometimes the reality yet always in the corporate world.

But of course, all humans are first the followers of their associations and then maybe few can learn to lead beyond them. (* see types of associations below)

- **Bhed**- stands for shared knowledge, information and using that to your advantage. This means being aware again of what drives others in your life. If you're aware of what the other person seeks like a position, role, knowledge, certification, anything tangible etc. you can offer that as a means to barter or better bargain your desired proposition. The knowledge of the enemy helps create common paths leading to lesser friction and perhaps respect and friendship in some case when the common purposes align.

Another great organizational behavior and career advice I got earlier on, that talks on the same lines as Chanakya's laws in our western world is Situational Leadership model for effective leaders.

Ken Blanchard and Paul Hersey developed the Situational Leadership Theory in 1969. The theory states that leaders should adapt their leadership style to the needs of their team or individual members in each situation. Blanchard's quote, "To bring out the best in others, leadership must match the development level of the person being led," summarizes the main concept of situational leadership.

Situational leadership is a flexible framework that provides a repeatable process for matching leadership behaviors to the performance needs of those being influenced. It involves:

- Identifying and analyzing team members' Performance Readiness factors

- Adjusting leadership style according to the maturity of the followers

- Creating a supportive environment where team members feel valued and motivated

The four leadership styles in situational leadership are:

S1: Directing/telling (high directive, low supportive think Tell someone to do a specific task to get a desired outcome.

S2: Coaching/selling (high directive, high supportive think Sell - like selling the idea to someone to do better to get rewarded and hence get to a desired outcome. Like sales incentives- or positive reinforcement. However, if you're not trained on what needs to be done- it's not going to matter if the rewards for higher target achievement is going to be higher- as you're not equipped (trained to meet the desired target in the first place hence rewards should not be the first step as it may be wasted.

S3: Supporting/participating (low directive, high supportive think Facilitate someone to do more than they're doing to enhance their skillsets and in turn improve team's performance. Like an older employee mentoring a new joiner

S4: Delegating (low directive, low supportive think Delegate to someone who's now independent contributor and is ready for higher responsibilities and role -you can delegate the specific tasks to still get a desired outcome.

In a nutshell- leadership is not set- it's an ongoing and diverse craft that can be honed by knowing your resources better to optimize productivity- in this case human resources. Each person will have an everchanging and evolving journey - both as a leader and a follower- based on their individual readiness levels and experiences. You can learn to adopt, adapt and change your approach based on where each member of your team is in their journey. It's not unheard of that each team has individuals across S1 to S4 and will need required unique tact to get managed effectively.

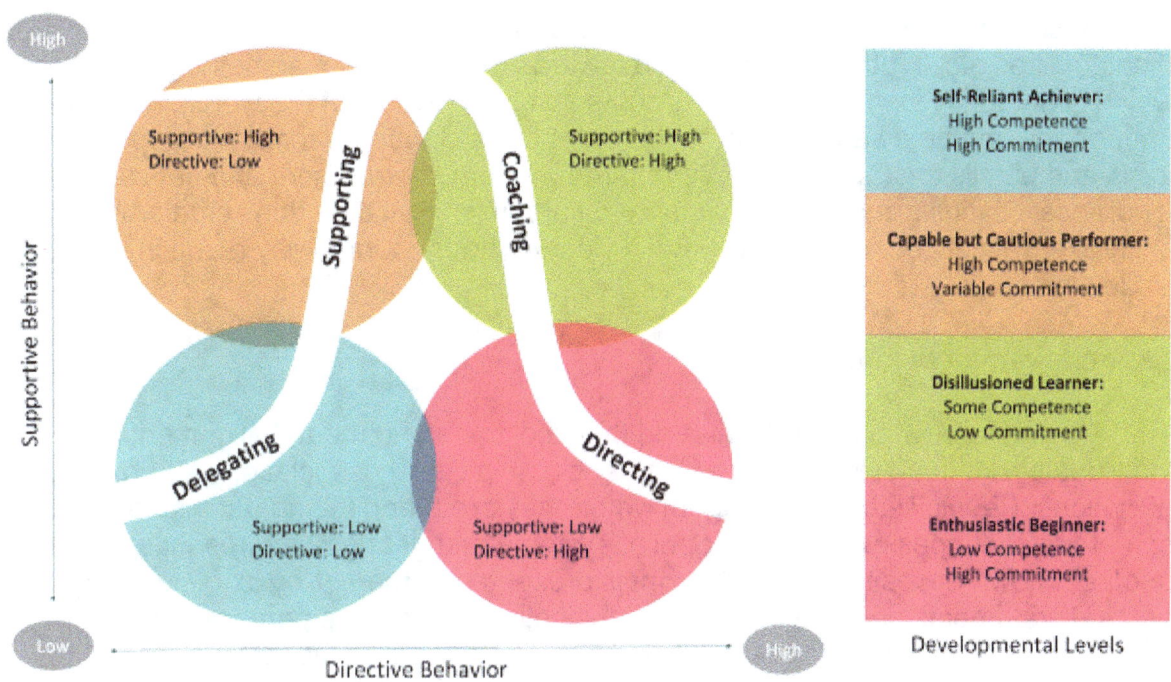

Types of Associations*:

Human beings are typically seen in 3 different types of associations in this world at a high level broadly. These are totally unique, and we all need to be aware of these to get favorable results and outcomes.

Here are the types of associations that we see in observation:

1. Associations of the Kind.

2. Associations of the Mind.

3. Associations of the Find.

While largely self-explanatory here's a simple definition for each.

Associations of the Kind-

This type of association centers around similarity on different subsets, caste, creed, color, religion, city, country etc. The fundamental principle is that like attracts like and people tend to cluster around their own kind of people, their kind of looks and their kind of taste, likes etc. in other words biased towards themselves or something familiar- which is natural. When speaking in group settings be aware of the words, demeanor, undertones and be aware of what're the acceptable standards for that group. Avoid traps and pitfalls to stay in favorable regards with the environment and not succumb to ignorance. Slangs are a disaster and are disappointing as they don't create win-win - as a speaker respect everyone or you will divide the house which may result in wanted issues later.

Associations of the Mind-

This type of association centers around the ideologies and mental alignments of the individuals- like book clubs or other literary clubs, political associations and religious affiliations. People listen more eagerly when they are tuned in and get aligned to something that goes well with their belief systems and get rigid and resentful whenever another known opposite idea or thought is presented to them. Key is to stay clear of general statements and use of any communication that maybe perceived threatening, confusing or even conflicting by anyone there. Faith is an individual journey and the best statement one can make in support of their belief in this world is to genuinely show the world your own wellness and unique gifts- drawing others to your way of thinking without having to say a word.

Associations of the Find-

This type of association talks about groups of people coming together or brought together based on their individual life paths and journeys- choices in day-to-day life- what relationships have survived the tests of times and how proximity or systemic alignments have resulted in a final unified bond and individuals associate together as one. Classic examples are organizations, companies, neighborhoods and gyms etc. While this is the most subtle one and most ignored- this is the most common one. People talk when they spend time together and this is a great place to open your minds and allow to learn and express, exchange fearlessly to one another. This will result in networking and create avenues for favors and better experiences and interactions. In other words, perhaps associations we find that our lifestyle allows. As most of our time will need us dealing with this association type (perhaps also in addition to one of the other 2 as well in some cases- like workplace)- knowing the individual's open associations is going to get well along with those groups and gel to create a favorable outcome. Also, this type of association is constantly changing in one's life.

The main reason to think in this regard is to gain more knowledge in to complex human mind and more empathy to create a better world for everyone to correlate and coexist meaningfully even if different.

Love is the absence of judgment- if you judge you will not be able to truly love. The answer is simple- allow and accept yourself and others to be unique and different.

As, what we care about or think about- grows. Including stress and negativity. We need to be very conscious of what we are thinking or associating with- daily diet makes up the body you live in- consume with awareness.

'Beyond the rightness or wrongness of things there is a field, I'll meet you there' -Rumi

Having a fresh perspective about things will feel free and the most important one to start with is to allow yourself to understand, enjoy and nurture your own self exploration. That you're enough and you're really what you need.

Ref: Psalm 23 -thou anointest my head with oil; my cup runneth over.

This is my interpretation of this verse from the bible (KJV - It talks about opening yourself to the higher one to anoint new learnings, experiences and episodes in your life with an awareness that with enlightenment and faith- one day you will be highly knowledgeable and prepared to lead this life with more abundance (my cup runneth over joy and happiness. Spreading and sharing your knowledge.

The new wine in the new wine holder.

I know this may be construed in religious connotation strictly for a few people who are not readers of the Bible- however even to them I say that the divine in its innumerable manifestations is the path laid down to enlightenment and is what humans seek to reach the highest level of their true potential in life or the said self-excellence.

This is also what Maslow's hierarchy talks about and some call the need for self-actualization.

If you believe God is in command- you're right. And if you believe you are the said God and are in command- you are right again.

Having faith sometimes means to carry an umbrella if rains in the forecasts and it's still sunny outside.

The path to real faith is when you practice every day even when no one's looking.

To push the point home, and if I have succeeded in making some of the readers wonder if this is a talk from the God channel or it's something they already know and may not agree with- I say - if you're on a path to self-excellence- faith is paramount in yourself (with or without a higher power).

Take care of your seconds and minutes, as they turn into hours, then days, then weeks, then years and finally your life.

Moving ahead on this path, to break away from the monotony and to seek more duration out of our days- look for spending time doing and being what makes you feel more confident and alive. If your job or current circumstances are testing, you- find an outlet to reflect the energies and come up as a stronger more reliable individual. End of the day having desires is a good thing and we should partake in non-regular activities regularly. This will allow you to avoid complacency and being redundant in your situation to create a new beginning that helps you dream of even better things for yourself and make positive contributions to the world in this lifetime.

Charity begins at home and so does cleanliness- It's important to understand that you're your first advocate/sponsor and friend. If you see yourself desiring others to be that for you- you're missing the point.

Your belief in everything comes from what you believe in- sometimes faith needs no company.

Here are a few things that will benefit you on the path to success and self-excellence:

- Seek time to spend on grooming how you carry yourself- it's strange that self-respect leads to everyone's respect.

- Seek time to spend time to stay fit. Learn to stay childlike and run outside. Apart from just sunshine - physical activities have proven to uplift your mood and willingness to try new things and grow.

- Good mental health is key if everything's mental and starts there. So truly strength and resilience is also mental before physical.

- Be a surprise- Yet a pleasant one- give people more than they can imagine making them think- breaking away from stereotypes and clichés has its own charm in life.

- Human beings are a creative species - in the absence of a relatable story- they create their own. If someone is already carrying something on their shoulders, they cannot pick up something else until they keep or let go of what they're already holding on to or carrying- same thing for your mindset and beliefs- we have to unlearn to learn- let go to hold on to something else. As simple as that.

- Understand weekday versus weekend topics for yourself and others. This is another key point to consider when doing the time management exercise.

- If you're working on your off days or not working on your workdays- there's something wrong.

- Acknowledge that you need to change and seek within the ways YOU can make your life more satisfying (to you).

- Make that change- whatever you want is on the other side of it.

Making changes now:

A good habit that I realized that helped me a lot is the freedom to scribble my thoughts and verbalize my learnings in simple sentences that I can relate to even later.

- Write as much as you can.

Another good tool is using every possible way to capture your thoughts and ideas (text, image, pictures, notepads, excel, word file, voice memos, etc.)

Spend time consciously to read what you have written and then change based on the latest. This will help create your unique style that's eloquent and precise for self-application or group improvements. With practice you will become better at it.

- Look to making an impact through your methods- share freely with anyone in need.

- Be supportive of others and stay humble.

- When praised stay confident when in disagreement stay civil.

- Always-think before you communicate- even more on calls/in face-to-face meetings

- When replying to an email- scribble the response then re-read it and refine again to make it sound more specific, genuine and non-judgmental. Doing this at least 2 times before clicking send will help avoid NVA exchanges and waste of time.

- When replying to any strong messages from your seniors, bosses or leadership- spend time to read exact message before you respond. I have found that we all have what I call the 'predictive preconceived response syndrome' - interestingly the predictions come from memory and most of the time - wrong. Let me give an example here, we get an email, and we already think we know what the sender is trying to say or suggest- in our mind we create a worst-case scenario and start from that place when we respond to it- mostly, as we know like gets like and we are drawn into a situation now which was not there an email before. So, take a breather, stay calm and read it again.

- Take a walk come back read it again and then try to reply specific to the point and not how you feel about it. I call it step away from the spreadsheet. Try it.

- In meetings, refrain from using too many Adjectives (ref: Adjectives are words that describe the qualities or states of being of nouns. They can also describe the quantity of nouns. For example, "a red dress" "real lazy" "southerners are like..." etc. These may help create the auditory impact for the listener however does not add anything real to the conversation. You want to be known for meaningful exchanges and not amusing conversations.

- To be a subject matter expert or the Master- you must behave like you already are- pretty much like 'Fake it till you make it". Because we are creatures of habit and what we do continuously, we believe.

- Observe other leaders and individuals that you're attracted to for their philosophy, style and purpose- and focus on what you see them do exceptionally well and then go ahead and do that.

- Always try to be 'to the point' - saves time.

- Allow people to take their time to respond- don't be too eager and needy. Constant follow up means that you're begging for attention more than probably what the topic means to everyone- cause if it's important and agreed expected- you will not need to follow up.

- However- if on constant follow ups you're not making any impact- go to the next person in the escalation matrix however be polite and keep it specific again to the topic and not about getting a response- This approach will help solidify your image as someone who can work the ranks and yet is unstoppable with their deliverables. And, that you're not a push over and are confident about your seat at the table.

- Be mindful though that every day you cannot escalate, and somethings will require you to think out of the box and use IM/Chat/phone call or setup a meeting invite with the said agenda proactively, to get your response as other ways to engage successfully. I have noticed these are more effective than escalations if you're required to work with the individuals on an ongoing basis.

- As a master storyteller, you need to be mindful. Get a structure in your thoughts and think before you reply.

- Always actively listen- sometimes there are no responses needed, so don't be too eager to answer back.

- Be very sure and think before you say Yes to anything as it's going to matter.

- Think even more if you say No - as it will matter even more.

Silent rules to ponder on:

- It's okay to Think that everyone other than you can be wrong- even desirable (most influencers have that self believe when compared to others and proven themselves right many a times) however please but don't say it to them even in jest.

- It's not too crazy to sometimes also think or feel that everyone's smarter than you- but remember to try even harder in that case. You will quickly learn and not have the feeling anymore.

- Lead by example- in meetings either prepare to lead or be open to be led without conflict. There's no room for feelings at the time of leadership.

- Use visual aid/data where possible but don't get drawn into rabbit holes and too many details and information- Data is only to support your analysis and on their own mean nothing. It's the message that needs to be focused on to create successful outcomes.

- Always have a good executive summary- like an elevator pitch ready. Most busy individuals like to talk to the point, concise, clear callouts and are not looking to self-absorb, learn explore or come up with what you're trying to say- present materials to support your pitch not drain through the materials. Aids are to aid not deliver the main message- you have to do that.

- Always overestimate risks- probability and quantification wise as its easier to go down than up.

- Enjoy today and each day- meetings, conferences and everything else included- you're not going to regret it.

- Start with a small plan to achieve and go from there.

- Sleep /Getup like clockwork with set wake up and sleep times. 7x365. (non-negotiable)

- Be aware of your health - finance/mental physical/emotional/stamina) attention/stress - and what drives these individually.

- Don't try to focus everything at the same time- remember prioritization and then dedicated focus is required else you will get overwhelmed easily and resign to mediocre beliefs and living.

- Respect the rule that family comes first- always.

- Learn to prioritize daily tasks and try to be happy by End Of the workday after completing your daily checklists of deliverables at work and then home.

- Set boundaries for everyone and for yourself - however be reasonable- respect is a two-way street- give and get it back.

When the going gets tough

- Review everything-if you're in a fix- spend time to understand the basics to complex.

- Demand the time that you need- better to be proactive than reactive.

- If you're hitting a mental wall or feeling tired or fatigue- step away and do something else-when you come back, review again with a new outlook.

- If you take a conscious and proactive approach and clearly and accurately break down Urgent versus Important tasks and then create a plan- you can handle anything. Sometimes taking a slow approach to success is better than rushing at high speeds towards disaster.

- In essence, really try to be the kindest and then also be the SMARTEST person in the room but don't try to prove it.

- Observe and be present "Pay" attention.

- Details are 'it'.

- Whatever the outcome- don't take it to your heart. There's nothing a good laugh with friends, family and good night's sleep can't fix. Next day start again- now you're starting with more context and perhaps a new perspective from experience.

- Focus on what if it works more than what if does not work. As it will- when you're ready.

- Keep it 'not personal' attitude if things don't work out for you.

- Keep it 'it's not permanent' attitude if things are working out for you.

- Don't avoid self-care - sharpen the saw. Rest, revive and refresh is the mantra.

Some tips to stay ahead of the curve.

- Plan your day/week ahead- start with small parts morning- afternoon and evening.

- Enjoy your seat at the table- take a moment to reflect on everything that you have done to reach the point you're at right now.

- Or on the floor (till you can get the seat on the table). Again, positive mental attitude.

- Remember that your problem has only one cure- you. Behave and allow yourself to behave like a true advisor - the elixir that can change the outcomes to be positive as it's got you in it now. You are what <u>you believe</u> you are- don't accept being a victim as an answer- make that change.

- When you're on the table or at least you're in the same room- be appreciative and try to play fair however don't expect the same from others and be naïve. Be alert and pay attention- this will either make your case or break it.

- Be genuine with people- say Thank you or if you need to apologies- be sincere.

- learn to share/make small talk-goes a long way. more

- Always have a cheerful demeanor- and smile more if on camera or in person. Your face should not show how you're feeling about it- poker face is an apt term here. Practice this skill as its hard to master but not impossible.

- Document everything proactively- minutes of meetings, discussions, agreed plan/owners/ dependencies, timelines anything that will help move ahead without confusion and conflict.

- Practice your plan - mirror technique has helped me many times in my jobs to be more impactful. Try it.

A larger life to live.

- Keep it simple- give Love receive Love. Giving attention to your potential is the highest form of love you can allow and give yourself.

- If you're adamant about not accepting anything half ass good or mediocre- you will see that you're only receiving the best- the key is to know and demand, what do you want.

- Invest in your dreams/ aspirations- you live this life once.

- Take support from others guilt free however aspire to return the favor when needed.

- Accept what happens and move on- even if you're out to change it.

- keep track of time- you may start wasting other's time and realize you end up wasting your own.

- Address ahead of time of what you cannot confidently predict in your professional outcomes at task/activity/ interaction level, however you can:

a) Try harder to learn/understand the fundamental principles that contribute to the overall design

b) Seek SME (subject matter experts) and other resources for help on helping you with any clarifications, doubts, and more importantly share best practices.

C) Look for Plan "B" approach that can work- there's always one- once you understand the fundamental principles, most often you will create one for yourself- believe in the power of relearning and practice.

d) Visualize the result favorably and recreate- retry.

- Celebrate uniqueness and differences- appreciating it will help you understand your audience a lot better.

- You can always 'Take it offline'- meaning discuss it again in a smaller group where the resolutions will be quicker.

- Preparation is the only key to success followed by prayer (self-belief)

The logic for victory is beyond pedigree and talent alone- it favors the brave- the one who's not deterred by situations and has practiced for hard knocks consistently.

Here's my favorite Bruce Lee saying.

"I fear not the man who has practiced 10,000 kicks. once, but I fear the man who has practiced one kick. 10,000 times." -Bruce Lee

This further confirmed my belief in preparation and practice- even to get lucky you must be consistent in your faith. One way or the other you're do just fine.

The Bruce Lee saying gave me a few insights:

1. Practice makes you excel on that thing

2. Practice makes others take notice of you and be feared for your mastery

3. To excel in one thing makes more sense than not being excellent in a lot of things- being specific helps.

There are other books that have helped me a lot- I highly recommend the ones I followed on my path and as I said earlier 7 habits is a great start.

7 habits of the highly effective people by Dr. Stephen Covey

The habits to develop as per Dr. Covey (and followed by corporates around the world in their LDP and MDP curriculums- I added it into each training and IDP across the firm in the Bank that I was responsible for all Organizational Development and talent framework back in 2005. I encourage you to read it at least twice.

The habits for a quick reference are (such a fan):

The 7 Habits of Highly Effective People®

1. Habit 1: Be Proactive®

2. Habit 2: Begin with the End in Mind®

3. Habit 3: Put First Things First®

4. Habit 4: Think Win-Win®

5. Habit 5: Seek First to Understand, Then to Be Understood®

6. Habit 6: Synergize®

7. Habit 7: Sharpen the Saw®

You should get familiar with the suggested techniques and use the tools recommended in this book to get more structured and organized on this path to self-excellence at the earliest.

I think at this point I want to get into the creation mode and share my experiences and lessons along the way.

In short, Yes- Law of attraction is a real thing- and that's the main problem in most cases, if you ask me.

Allow me to explain here, at a high level the entire physical world is governed by just 1 thing alone eventually, everything else is just leading into that or is an outlet of those frequencies. It's called 'Vibrations'.

While it's an entire study on its own -in a very simple way said, in my understanding, our being as an individual or even as a part of a larger collective being group called humankind, we have something called an aura. This is the net vibration that we operate on at an existential level and varies from time to time. These vibrations or frequencies at which operate in our day to day are a result of the 'energy' we carry and use- sounds, movements and most importantly the thoughts we FEEL. So, think if every man on this planet as an energy meter grid say on a scale of 1- 10 - and 1 means miserable and 10 is bliss- each thought generates a specific level on the scale. Now think the cumulative individual score gets added to a Total number for everyone in that environment. That total is what defines what we also refer to as the vibe of that place, person or event (collection of people in a place).

While feelings are natural, they usually stem from past experiences and a flight response generally associated with the time spent in this life in a very crude way.

Life has other universal principles that govern it all- as agreeable and common as the Law of Gravity.

As an average, everyone with enough time given, will have a life that in some areas will have an experience in extremes either 1 or 10- finally netting it out for everyone as a score.

However, what we can do is to start controlling our thoughts and in effect the vibrations we are creating through our feelings. So, we can allow feelings to happen however we can control the thoughts that are causing the said feeling and if addiction is what the chemical brain craves- deliberately think things that will resonate feelings of immense pleasure and abundance in place of poverty, limitations and ill-health - pretty much rigging the system in our favor. Over a period, it'll be as natural as breathing- again something we should all do naturally effortlessly all the time.

While this sounds so simple- the barrier is the law of attraction.

I realized our negative thoughts have as much impact if not less and in fact they're like feistier, in choice of better words, and will grab more attention unless dealt with completely by you. I say that knowingly as that's what needs to happen- as we think more consciously- our mind starts to calm down and creating nonexistent situations to freak out on. Over time effortlessly.

Remember, as humans- in the absence of a reason, we creatively make our own-when we feel good the mind starts to relax and not create scenarios that have a conflict response creating a positive 'vibe' or just the opposite.

Now let's address the concept of attraction.

Attraction as a force "In physics, attraction is the force by which things are pulled toward each other. For example, magnets attract iron filings".

When you notice a magnet at work- the opposite polls attract and this can create a powerhouse of pull is many pieces come together, creating a much larger pull- keep this in mind.

This is also loosely reference on a very fundamental yet powerful law- called polarity. In a lay man term- Polarity is the scale of attraction from -ve to +ve again this is not something that I have scientifically proven myself however have felt it many a times to believe in it. Once we can get our focus aligned to bringing the positive vibe to the table- we will attract similar vibes and create more such aura.

Another- way to understand this as I see is- if you can motivate yourself from within and start maintaining a said calm frequency- staying calm as still as you can be- chances are that the hypnotic control of your charisma (consisting of aura gives charisma) will help you weave and create a world that you're now also physically living.

As H2O - every time we mix atoms of Hydrogen with Oxygen, we will get Water- Ice, steam, condensation, etc. when we apply this to our thoughts to feelings to vibrations- we get the same result predictable and proven.

Once we understand that the real world is inside and we have a say in what happens to us we start breaking down the knowledge (I still don't know why it is masked and openly shared, anyway and start to apply it in our day-to-day life- making the law work for us on demand. This leads us to redefine and to replant our thoughts, after all at the beginning everything is mental- a desire, a thought which we are thinking- nothing less and nothing more.

Control your thoughts - else they will control you.

Another thing to observe now is the sound I earlier spoke about- every sound can also be confined to the vibrations it creates. If we shout and cry in rage our frequency is very low however our vibration is jarring. Remember this- your physical health and being will stem from your mental being- stop raising your voice. Also stop using negative words- words that hurt and not heal. If you're looking for a cheat code, here's one- be very and I mean very conscious of the words that you're saying- even in Jest. Energies don't have a sense of humor.

Reference Bible – "John 1:1 In the beginning was the Word, and the Word was with God, and the Word was God."

Your words will start everything- don't go on a self-inflicted destruction rampage by exaggerating and creating a larger than real image of things and situations in your mind before they happen in real life- you're unknowingly creating your own reality by talking. This I realized was one of the main fundamental principles and needs respect and needs to be guarded closely.

So now that we have established thoughts and words (sound create your vibrations and in turn your overall aura- and that we can control how we feel by switching our thoughts and words- we are closer to finding the key to life and let's say the talismans that can help make our dreams a reality. We create the outcome with faith as we wish endlessly.

The Law of attraction is further explained as a manifestation of dreams or aspirations. Now these can either through clear set goals, say like being a successful businessperson or an actor; Or just plain wishful thinking, say like winning a lottery to the road to abundance. Whatever you do believe- stick with it and have the faith.

This law has no judgement hence it's so powerful that whatever we start to believe we start to manifest and see.

Reference Bible Matthew 7:7-8-King James Version

"*7 Ask, and it shall be given you; seek, and ye shall find; knock, and it shall be opened unto you:*

8 For everyone that asketh receiveth; and he that seeketh findeth; and to him that knocketh it shall be opened."

Even Jesus Christ affirms that the word will lead you to your destiny- again these are my interpretations and not the only way to be understood.

In short, never underestimate the power of small things- they make up the big things.

Tips for managing stupid.

- Many a times while you're working on your Aura and creating a positive personal vibe- don't ever ignore the power of stupid.

- In most group business settings presumptions and assumptions will create confusion to derail even the most prepared details. I call it the power of stupid- add a bad vibe and poor choice of words and you have a recipe for downward spiral and everything chaos.

- Here's how to work with this- yes, work.

- Understand the level of subject matter expertise and knowledge, or experience whatever you want to call it is your audience- new customers, old customers, promoters, detractors, friends alliances - you get the drift.

- Now when you're story boarding make sure you try to callout the specifics that the group is interested in- with time and repetition you will be able to get adrift of how it goes in said situations- most people are not creative (sad but true) and you will see patterns and based on their perception of who they are, their natural aura (how you feel about them as a starter) and the various hypothesis that they can bring to the meetings. Take notes.

- To plan for stupid- don't get alarmed with anything nothing is out of bound in this world- just stay calm and try to get to a simpler agreement.

- When you take notes- you're learning from your past Fuck ups.

- People are unique- their thoughts/actions have a pattern-study. All the time- even more study and reflect on how you responded and what outcome did you get. Think like a video game- the more you play the more you get better.

- Don't be lazy all the time. Cannot emphasis how important is to plan your day- you're one step closer to the goal or one step down the drop.

If you're the smartest person in the room- you probably are in the wrong room. Get out now-addiction will drag you to a room full of no good admirers. (addiction is the rush from the room of fools treating you different, yet mediocre)

Arguably, I realized most people are so caught up in their own lives- they don't really have the time to give a thought or a fuck.

So let me tell you a story now - about Dronacharya and his student Eklavya who he did not teach from the Hindu mythology.

I like the story as it's really real and confirms my believe in the art of war and the power of practice even more.

Here's the story in short.

"In the Mahabharata, the story of Eklavya and Dronacharya is about a poor hunter named Eklavya who wants to learn archery from Dronacharya, a renowned teacher of archery.

Dronacharya refuses to accept Eklavya as a student because he is not of noble birth and his Gurukul is meant for princes and royal children.

Eklavya is determined and does not complain when Dronacharya rejects him. Instead, he becomes a self-taught archer by watching Dronacharya teach others and creating a clay statue of Dronacharya as his guru (teacher).

Eklavya eventually becomes the most skilled archer through hard work and willpower."

The story of Eklavya and Dronacharya includes several morals, including:

1. Practice makes perfect: Eklavya wasn't born with archery talent, but he practiced hard and became very good at it.

2. Self-mentoring: Eklavya achieved his goal by teaching himself.

3. Dedication and resilience: Eklavya was denied training by Dronacharya, but he became the best archer through his determination and dedication.

4. Never be afraid to start from scratch: Eklavya started from scratch and became the best archer.

5. Respect your elders: Eklavya's story emphasizes the importance of respecting elders.

6. Passion: Eklavya's passion and devotion are what count, not just in his professional life but also in his personal life.

Another quote from Julius Ceasar that I can talk about here that magnifies learning is:

"Decius Brutus: If he be so resolved, I can oversway him, for he loves to hear that unicorns may be betrayed with trees, lions with toils and men with flatterers. But when I tell him he hates flatterers, he says he does, being then most flattered".

Or my interpretation of it-"They say Julius Ceasar hates flattery but when they say Julius Ceasar hates flattery- Julius Ceasar is Flattered".

The point is that everyone loves flattery - and to some perhaps it's the highest form of flattery to be copied or imitated. Look for such available mentors who you can learn, copy and develop your style on. Now if you're truly standing out and say that you don't want to copy, you can try to understand the reasons and mannerism that makes the other person successful and excellence. Not everyone's your competition and even if you think they're, learn from them to better yourself.

Introduction to the 'Interpretation principles'

Awareness to these principles will help you navigate through the outcomes and decisions a lot faster. Here's a list of principles that impact individual interpretations - or how they perceive things:

- Individual Conditioning

- Social background

- Trust in the relationship,

- Past experiences,

- Mental orientation

- Social income profile,

- Social strata

- Personal associations (we spoke about this earlier),

- Income class,

- Individual conduct

Now what?

Spend some time to talk to people and understand what drives them and what makes them click. Again, build rapport.

The more you can understand yourself and others the easier it gets to work with them and then goals are just numbers.

Some rules for meetings that can help:

- Be aware of your audience and group setting- a lot of its evident rest can either be researched on social media or assimilated with experience over time.

- In a meeting, either agree or disagree and if required explain why.

- And, if you are neither here nor there, don't bother to bring it up- lay low till you can decide.

- Always, always-ask questions- even to confirm your understanding of the matter.

- Again, keep professional/Personal separate and do not mix. If someone likes you don't bend over and if someone dislikes you- don't go guns baring.

- Respect both parallel universes- one as you're seeing based on your perception and one perhaps that's what's actually happening. (So don't get passionate about your own understanding alone- air it to clear it.)

- Plan for both worlds as they unfold.

- Always write inputs else forget and lose it.

- If you forgot - it'll mostly mean a penalty to pay. Think you have a limited water supply, and you left the tap on and forget- bound to create some discomfort- deal with it.

- Risks = dividends (calculated risks mean what you can manage through your experience and practice- you have done it before)

- Results result in relationships and net worth = impact

- Remember when working in groups-there are no silos, you're in the same team.

- Be prepare to lift the layers by asking fact finding questions and set rapport.

- Don't be secretive- Everyone needs to know- information is power- if you're providing information- you're powerful.

- To develop foresight and strategic thinking play chess and learn to meditate.

- If you're new and you don't understand the organization totally- learn, observe and ask questions to decide.

- Always check your tone/ body language in each interaction, this is what will bring conflicts otherwise.

- If you have no lessons yet in life- like starting out really young- prepare it's going to be hard however if you are open it's going to be fine and fun.

- However hard the pain, please remember- pain is a response mechanism and it teaches us a lesson to avoid repeat offence- focus on the cause and lesson (affect).

- If you're looking carefully-there are no surprises in life. And definitely no coincidences.

Well- except nature- it can surprise you. If you're ever in the Bay area CA- one minute its sunshine and next it rains.

Some observations along the way:

- Successful outcomes in communication comes from being a better facilitator them a good speaker- ask others to talk.

- To hold attention is the key yet don't hog the Prime time /Limelight

- Learn to reflect & deflect for solutions to arrive naturally from the group unanimously- golden phrases- what do you think? How do you see it come together?

- Either you ask or stay ignorant.

- Ignorance is not bliss in professional life; unlike personal where we don't really want to know too much to avoid judgement.

- Feedback helps get better.

What we know about ourselves versus what people think about us.

Let me introduce you to the concept of Johari's window. It goes something like this, the Johari Window is a model that helps people improve self-awareness and self-communication. It's a communication model that describes how people perceive themselves and how others perceive them.

The Johari Window was published in 1955 and is named after its inventors, Joseph Luft and Harry Ingham.

The Johari Window is divided into four quadrants:

1. Open: Information that is known to both the individual and others

2. Blind: Things you don't know about yourself, but others do

3. Hidden: Things you know about yourself, but keep hidden

4. Unknown: Things that are unknown to you and to others

The Johari Window is a valuable tool for understanding personality. It relies on feedback and communication, which helps ground perception in the experience of others.

The Johari Window Model:

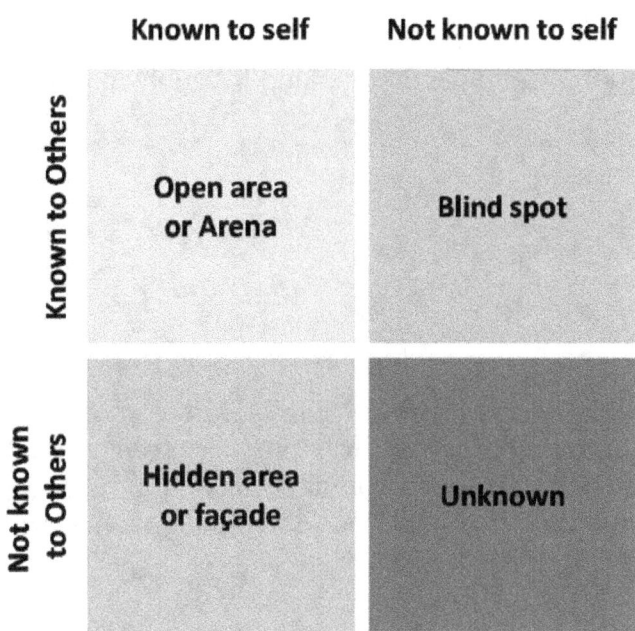

The Johari Window Model

This is important for any growth mindset individual to know- to be self-aware and more importantly help understand what we already don't know about ourselves- after all it's a journey of self-exploration and finally excellence- to be the best version of ourselves.

In general, always, always, call people by their names. Creates an instant connection.

Try humor/Jest if you can afford to.

Also Know when not to jest.

Be human and be patient both others and with yourself.

In a discussion, either help others 'on board your train of thoughts' or get onboard theirs's - cannot go undecided.

Take a point of view, explore it till the end and then move ahead.

Be prepared for days that don't feel good- in short, give room to hormones- they will need space and time.

Solution contingency planning and risk quantification is the 'making it doubly sure part' - do it well.

Here are some tips:

- Always have a FMEA or Failure mode effect analysis or a Control plan for your business- these statistical tools help mitigate and arrive at probable risks coming from the nature of the environment and their associated severity impact to come up with an overall quantified outcome. Then recommending potential and tested mitigation tools and remedy levers to control and eliminate the defect.

- Spend time seeking feedback from as many sources as you can- more from your direct contacts. This will help you do an unbiased SWOT analysis. Know your' strengths weakness, opportunity areas and threats' to further your strategy and get more efficient with yourself.

SWOT Analysis:

- To explain further- everyone has unique strengths. And then they also have certain weaknesses. There are also some areas of opportunity for improvement and lastly there are traits that can be a threat to you. Being aware of these things about your own self will help you do conscious control and act as a measure to keeping you aligned to constantly 'Prepare for your - WOT. While you successfully focus and practice your 'S' (strengths).

- If in an environment where performance management is graded - always play to overachieve Outstanding/ Exceeds Expectation and not Meets Expectations.

- End of the day relationships matter- invest in them wisely.

- The best relationships you can have is when you start with yourself. Spend time with yourself alone.

- Remember to build trust and create an effective relationship - say what you mean and mean what you say. And be genuine in your responses.

After all, trustworthiness is nothing else but past experiences and memories of them. How did they feel about it if it has happened before.

People will behave and judge you based on their 'past experiences with you or others.

How to create agreeable and meaningful experiences consciously.

- Know your data and the accuracy of it.

- Get consent from everyone on the same including, glossary, definitions, dependencies and meaning.

- Always try to arrive at basic metrics to translate into bottom line - that can be easily agreed on.

- Remember, if it's easier to understand, easier to explain then it's easier to implement.

- Key principle is that everything measured can be improved- you can test it.

- Start with defining the Measurement Systems based on the common understanding before you start measuring.

- Be ready to be the' No'/ Ask difficult questions type of person if you don't understand, even if it means more work for you.

- In a meeting, go with the flow if you need to plan - ask for time ahead of the meeting or after.

- Important to Start and End the meetings on time. Makes an impact.

- Be patient with yourself and others, if that fails one time and you lose it- try even harder next time.

- If you're the host of the meeting show up a few min sooner.

- If you're the worker bee- think you're the host- meaning- be prepared to take the lead as you're the one who's going to have to work.

- If you're the reviewer be on time.

- And if you're late as a reviewer-explain why.

- Block your Calendar proactively to manage your time - even lunch breaks.

- Be your own customer first and evaluate how did you do?

- Advocate for yourself how you would for others (rationally)

- Take risks sometimes but always calculate and quantify first.

- Invest and check your mental health-consciously every now and then, How am I feeling right now. Breathe.

- Remember If you take the lead in creating the overall plan for the team, you're actually starting at pole position. Initiatives and self-start habits go a long way to mastery.

- When in between a hard place and a rock situation-

Follow 3 steps of caution to proceed: -

1. Check Emotion
2. Check Body language / Tone.
3. Check vocabulary.

If what you're about to say will ignite more than unite → Say nothing. Accept feedback.

- While you quantify rational versus personality based on the individual's feedback> keep rational alone, let go any personality portions and stay on topic.

- Ask specifics like what type / template/ table/ flow, etc. to reply to tasks. End in mind.

- Remember 'show me vs tell me' Audiences as you plan your response.

- Know the difference in both approaches- one will get excited with details and exploration journey with you the other will like to know key messages and callouts driven from all the details known.

- Always think before you respond to direct questions.

- Try to re-evaluate and re-assess as many times as possible that you like, to once more try by paraphrasing.

- Emails are tricky if you don't agree/understand -slow down and step away. Come back and reapply your focus slowly and then reply-still don't press send-review in sometime again and then if satisfied-click send.

- I can't emphasize the importance of not immediately replying to emails- we all are guilty of reading sometimes based on our preconceived notions and make mistakes easily. Be aware.

- Even if urgent take your time to review and then send- don't get rushed- go on DND- do not disturb, if needed...

- Focus on growth (internal & External) as the driving principle.

- Reevaluate and jot down your short term and long term 'goals.'

- Know the difference between' goals' and 'aspirations' and 'dreams' also 'wishful thinking' so you can prepare accordingly.

- Deserve and then desire (see yourself-as deserving-will happen over time, if you' work on yourself) prepare for it and then you can desire as you please.

- Living Mon-Fri for Sat/Sun is not a bad idea if you think about it. stay consistent through changes and watch yourself grow. In short, take small steps daily.

In an abstract way, think of your worst fears coming alive and you're being chased by them continuously, what do you do? There may be limited choices if being chased- either you run fast or you turn around and fight- but always remember to run fast first.

We need to keep in mind- a lot of pain, stress and anxiety is caused by our unnecessary speaking- not having a conflicting attitude is a desired trait in humans- giving too much into friction and retaliation is against law of attraction at work- as like begets like.

A master knows his path and does not show too much emotion.

'When someone beats a rug, the blows are not against the rug, but against the dust in it. - Rumi'

Lessons to learn:

- Don't try to outsmart, try to collaborate and engage-work, together starts with you.

- Use 'work together' effectively if you want to succeed. Even the phrase has a positive feel.

- Define success in your life' timeline' give daily outcomes and outputs importance- seed to fruit takes time and both nature and nurture. And enjoy, celebrate each small step towards growth.

- Learn to challenge yourself first-really hard for over 90% human beings as we seek comfort over logic- however now we're seeking excellence the other end of the spectrum so get used to being uncomfortable.

- Challenging yourself comes with being honest and worthy of the feedback people and life gives you - if you're listening attentively.

- Adjectives are not feedback- don't take it too personally.

- When you get a candid feedback-ACCEPT IT!

If you keep pushing back, you're delaying the process of alignment and your own journey.

- Questions make people nervous - some more than others. Still ask them but change the way you ask them. A few times in my career I was told that I ask too many questions- which I always found interesting as asking questions makes you smarter as you're thinking ahead and being innovative.

Curious minds have a thirst for knowledge. I did slow down a bit and started asking only pointed ones (without building up to the key question as taught by some sales academies- anyway, questions that help you to get at the minimum whatever information is needed to create responsibly as a master business solution architect.

- Once you have done your due diligence, validation or diagnostics- whatever you want to call it, you will be able to decide and know what needs to be done-do it, at least try once then next time try again harder with experience.

A very common mistake is to give up doing the right thing because others don't agree. To stand out, be ready to stand alone.

- Be aware and beware of your tone and also of your audience- short and sweet when in doubt with clear takeaways and actions from that interaction.

- Life is daily- think, feel bad, cry if you have to then move ahead- as you can't eat on one day for the rest of your life- neither can you for your dreams- you have to do piece by piece everyday go with the flow. We live daily.

- Look back at all the things that you have survived to this point in your life- you have survived. Celebrate.

- Assess your weaknesses first however do not forget the lessons learnt and enjoy your experiences with fame as it unfolds. After all, success starts in your backyard.

- Seek to further enhance your strengths to mastery-and opportunities-accept the truth and 'work on yourself'.

3rd person perspective

- Try visualizing or writing (truthfully) or record yourself talking about anything -then analyze with a 3rd person perspective

- Remember, in business as in life, outcome is everything and result oriented Ness- if there's disagreement, failure, stress or an argument of any kind then - it's not good- work more selflessly to get consensus and harmony.

- No matter who's fault it is, as the master to be- you do what's needed.

- If the outcome gives happiness - do more of that. If not, do it right and get done with it.

- We cannot control outcomes however we can start with a good one from the start consciously.

- Be positive and optimistic about the outcome and work back from there.

- Learn to be diplomatic and tactful- it keeps countries from war.

- Create win-win in your daily interactions so everyone is eager to be around you.

- Try to be responsible however do not try to control anything.

- Learn to live in parts and not let whole be one. No one thing, deal, day or event should be assumed as final. Move ahead with your head held high and try more next time, tomorrow.

- Everyone does not dislike you-neither does everyone they like.

- Be reasonable, others don't owe you anything neither do you! If no one gives a fuck- then why do you...

- Emotions are chemicals going through a change, ongoing- keep them in check by being aware- nothing else is needed- remember what we measure is what we can change.

- Don't push-pull will work in your favor - unless you're holding a snake then push away.

- Create' Dependability' - if everyone can do it then you're no special- it works both ways if you're special then others won't do- they need you.

- Follow creative avenues to get outcomes and desired results- don't just do if that's how it's always been done.

- Re-evaluate. value to effort is the main metric in everything -ask if it is worth it?

- Don't do everything learn to delegate what's easier to control- however the accountability is still yours.

- If cutting grass is on your list -and you don't enjoy working at your day job and have to cut grass-get someone to help-pay them to cut grass and go to work for you to get paid. Some people take everything on their plates and don't finish anything. Remember value to costs in each transaction.

- Just evaluate cost of yourself vs others AND execute.

- STOP Ponzi scheming yourself - Be real with yourself and stop telling yourself whatever that you do that tries to justify your being in your situation is due to your circumstances, economy or the world- it's not true.

- Have things to worry about-yet be real don't worry about everything at once.

- Watch your thoughts as thoughts turn into feelings.

- Like everything in life - the ending matters.

- Think running an animal farm.

- At the farm consistency is key. Discipline is required. No surprises is the routine and is important. Such is with social animals.

- Remember a farm/ranch life is like a business and due diligence and conscious effort is required with perseverance. If you can also do physical labor - you're already in the lead- maintain it.

- Nothing - Nothing trumps preparation and hardwork.

- Keep in mind, even a small thing can trigger a big event.

- Avoid **'mono math' complex- only one way of thinking**- you're allowed to change your perspective and even opinions.

- Don't say everything you want to- even if you think you can. Even if You're right.

- Trust nature as that's the real world happening- pay attention to being. Breathe.

- Mental health is the only health that needs 'Consciousness' real time. It's not a sign or symptom it's the overall wellbeing.

- Depression is Real time too - living in the past is the main reason.

- Making journals/goal sheets plans/ ideas and talking about life outside of work and allowing self to do those things are a great tool to balance your moods.

- Being in nature helps as we are a part of nature.

- Creating positive' mindsets' on the way it can be done and where to find help- helps!

- If there are miscommunications, misunderstanding and clear gaps- taking a few steps back with clarity on discreet data (limited to yes/no) helps (not continuous data like numerical or maybe or something, someone, etc.).

- However, for specifics use data like date/time who/what when/Where/ documented. The key here 'to get to the point of common consensus unanimously and then pave forward to the desired conclusion. Numbers in this regard are specific and fixed.

- Remember 'Vague begets vague'. Keep it simple.

"If a man knows not to which port he sails, no wind is favorable" is a quote by Seneca

- Clearly calling out specifics and outcomes, owners, timelines, milestones and proper planning helps.

- Next assign action owners mapping to each deliverable with timelines.

- Keep yourself and others honest based on progress of each owner regularly.

- Distraction is the curse driven from the advancement of technology- be aware, check for understanding and consensus before you close out. Just don't say yes or no without really understanding the asks.

- Showing up is the key. Even on not so good days.

- Seek feedback and if possible, follow up later.

- Getting the team to work is also work -sometimes more.

- Be ready to demand attention. Hence no distractions are there to stop you from meeting your desired goal for the hour/day/week.

- Analysis to paralysis is the fundamental challenge on staying on topic and stick to the agendas in most meetings. Again, distractions drive the gap (in understanding) to achieve end results- be creative and keep it short and simple.

- Make a work plan -documentation is reality- make it the saw/ sword. And sharpen the saw consistently.

Let's all strive for Combined Cumulative Consciousness (CCC) – we are all connected at the ether. What you feel everyone does.

- Ego is a barrier; instead of 'I am Smart' it's we're smarter together.

The Application of CCC is going to unleash a new powerful human race, unleashing energies to flow freely and uplift the new- in this reality – be sure that you are not contributing to the stress.

Somethings to remember:

- Emaul - emails can maul- don't be an eMauler- the old-school hard-handed task masters are not going to flourish in this new age. So, learn something new while you still can.

- Excellence is a phase arrived by proactive and innovative mindsets.

- Show up, even if it's not your choice. shows strength of character and leadership.

- Practice your choices more openly.

- Summarize before agreeing and disagreeing. What you do is governed by that.

- Whenever you're bringing in any changes to the status quo there'll be resistance-pull is as helpful as push.

- Easier to set their minds to seek by planting ideas to explore then force your own.

- The only evident way to be witnesses to the event at play is to assimilate how are you feeling and what is the mood/ Energy around you. Adapt accordingly.

- Being calm avoids delay caused by chaos.

- To win a game you must play it. How you win is an outcome of how you play- with love, luck or need.

- You can fool some of the people all the times; all of the people' sometimes '- however you cannot fool yourself. If you're not good at something and are required to do it and are facing consequences or energy surges; it's because you're not respecting the task and giving in the required time, patience and effort. Spend the time to learn and practice.

- Any addiction is driven by the habit or act of consumption and does not have an individual existence of its' own.

- Explain well don't try to convince (or convert).

- To avoid conflict-think before you speak and edit before you press send.

- Once you proofread and the general tone is collaborative, respectful, and to the point- it helps.

- Adjectives and expletives don't contribute to logic- data does. Avoid descriptions.

- Energy is the key to communication.

- Accepting other's perspectives doesn't reduce yours.

- Cultivate discipline yet try not to form habits.

- Travel physically, mentally, spiritually to learn about emotionally.

- Seek to understand before you seek to be understood. (7 habits)

- If you want inspiration look around, if you want Ideas, look within.

- In itself, Magic is nothing, if you don't believe.

- The best way to focus on anything-disjoint completely from everything else.

- Remember no one knows or can really know others completely, and no one cannot not Know themselves completely- if they try.

- People are either happy to see you come or relieved when you go/leave. pay attention.

- Win hearts/moods not conversations.

- The flip side of mic drop' is no more communication.

- Don't take a tank to a fistfight.

- Breathe often, yet consciously- totally aware of your environment; either you're inside/out or outside out.

- Talk to yourself as you do with other and talk to others about you.

- Why thieves succeed, and teachers don't -they visualize the end plan. -what a mind can conceive, and the tongue can perceive that's what will be eventually achieved.

- **Everyone** chants mantras-be watchful of what you chant (say out loud often).

- We live in our minds hence it is the most important place to be looked after.

- Thoughts and feelings manifest the physical being, health and diseases.

- Panic is the manifestation of out of sync between different departments (thought, speech, action and PURPOSE)

- Many a conflict can be resolved if words are known for their vibration more than their perceived meaning and association. Battles are fought because of this one discord. Be careful not to get confused by words.

- Seek to know the world and explore yourself.

- Meditation is the ploughing of thoughts, awareness, consciousness and is always, ongoing-not a small silent session.

- Through action comes meditation.

- Selflessness stems from actions without expecting outcomes.

- To change negativity, think positive-however to receive you have to give.

- If you don't accept, you don't receive-good/Bad

- If someone gives you grief, don't take it.

- Manage your consciousness to guide your subconscious.

Lastly, remember as the saying goes- It's not over till it's the end and it's not the end till it's over.

Go in faith- love conquers all- start with loving yourself now.

****

A huge THANK YOU, to everyone who challenged me and made my life difficult- because of you I became so good at what I do.

In poetic juxtapose on a lighter note-

'To all my enemies and competitors,

I am so glad we met; I see a huge part of you in me.

And now that you know, look within and I am sure you will see a huge part of me. Till next time'

- Ajay Solomon

www.ingramcontent.com/pod-product-compliance
Lightning Source LLC
Chambersburg PA
CBHW082217220526
45470CB00010B/3205